We Refugees

Edited by Emma Larking

Pact Press

Published by Pact Press
An imprint of
Regal House Publishing, LLC
Raleigh, NC 27612
All rights reserved

https://pactpress.com

ISBN -13 (paperback): 9781947548343
Library of Congress Control Number: 2019941442

Interior and cover design by Lafayette & Greene
lafayetteandgreene.com
Cover image © by Alex Johnson, 'Rescue in the Mediterranean' from the ten image set, 'My Voyage from Nigeria to Italy.'

Regal House Publishing, LLC
https://regalhousepublishing.com

Printed in the United States of America

For those in search of safety, hope, and home—
that you may know you are not alone.

CONTENTS

"We are all story. That's what my people say. From the moment we enter this physical reality to the moment we depart again as spirit, we are energy moving forward to the fullest possible expression of ourselves. All the intrepid spirits who come to this reality make the same journey. In this we are joined. We are one. We are, in the end, one story, one song, one spirit, one soul."

- Richard Wagamese, *One Story, One Song*

WE REFUGEES

Emma Larking

"We Refugees" is the title of an essay written in America in 1943 by the German Jewish philosopher, Hannah Arendt.[1] Like many of Hitler's exiles who escaped to the United States, Arendt felt tremendously grateful to the country for affording a place of safety, yet "We Refugees" is not a tale of gratitude. The essay is difficult to read: it makes you shift restlessly in your chair. It is written in a sardonic tone of voice, and there is bitterness in it. Arendt's critical attention touches on those offering refuge—the good citizens of America—and also focuses on the refugees themselves.

The Americans offered safety, but with a sting. The refugees were expected to blend into their new society as quietly and submissively as possible. They were beleaguered by constant reporting requirements and forms to fill in. On the West Coast they were treated as "enemy aliens" and subject to nightly curfews, but their hosts implied that all these measures were imposed reluctantly, in a spirit of friendship, and any comparison to how the refugees had been treated by the Nazis was most unwelcome.

---

[1] Except where otherwise noted, all quotes come from Hannah Arendt [1943] "We Refugees" in Mark M. Anderson (ed), *Hitler's Exiles: Personal Stories of the Flight from Nazi Germany to America*, New York, USA: The New Press, 1998.

As for the refugees themselves: they didn't like to be called refugees but preferred "newcomers" or "immigrants" or even "Americans of German language." They had been "so unfortunate as to arrive in a new country without means," and had to rely on the assistance of "Refugee Committees," but despite their difficulties they were "very optimistic" and commenced their new lives by trying, Arendt says, "to follow as closely as possible all the good advice [their] saviors passed on to [them]," including to forget quickly their old lives. In light of this advice,

> they avoided any allusion to [the] concentration or internment camps [that they had] experienced in nearly all European countries – it might be interpreted as pessimism or lack of confidence in the new homeland…how often [they] had been told that nobody likes to listen to all that…Apparently nobody wants to know that contemporary history has created a new kind of human being – the kind that is put in concentration camps by its foes and in internment camps by its friends.

Arendt's description of the refugees who were expected to keep their mouths shut and to avoid causing offence, even when this meant ignoring rather unpalatable political facts, is disconcerting. These were resilient and brave people who had weathered terrible events. Yet despite this, there is acid in the way that Arendt describes how many of the refugees in America took to reading their future in horoscopes, while others resorted to suicide—in her words: "having made a lot of optimistic speeches, [they] go home and turn on the gas or make use of a skyscraper in quite an unexpected way."

Rather than be offended by Arendt's account, it should spur contemporary readers to reconsider common portrayals of what is widely referred to as the current "refugee crisis." Often these portrayals ignore the agency and individuality of forced migrants. Where they are sympathetic, they are full of pathos, but rarely do they focus on the hard issues of why people are leaving their homes and risking their lives. They almost never address how policies pursued by wealthy States —including arms sales to authoritarian or autocratic regimes, preferential trade deals, and refusals to relieve crippling sovereign debt burdens—may be implicated in the situations that push people into exile.

Rather than be alienated by what seems like an attitude of derision in Arendt's essay, we need to read it in light of what she wrote elsewhere about the human condition, and what it means to build political communities together with other human beings. For Arendt, to be human is to have agency in the world. It is the capacity to influence the shape of the world that we construct and share with other human beings who are our equals.

When the scale of a problem seems to defy comprehension or our ability to respond effectively, it can be tempting to surrender responsibility and resort instead to a focus on our inner or personal lives: putting our trust in fate or the stars, or else surrendering all trust and hope and considering suicide the only way out.

What Arendt is urging on her readers is the imperative of action in common with like-minded people and in defence of communities of hope and empowerment. If we abandon the political stage and the sphere of public policy making, surrendering it to those who make policy in pursuit of power or vindictive and vicious world views, all hope for a better shared future is lost.

Refugees have been forced to flee their homes and countries. They seek safety or shelter or simply a crust of bread where their home offered none. They request entry to, and participation in, a new political community. But refugees need not, indeed they should not, be cowed as a result of this. Nor should they be expected to scrape and bow to their hosts in other countries, encouraged like feudal beggars to offer thanks for stale crusts tossed away from an aristocrat's feast.

Who are we, those of us fortunate enough to be seated at the table, to claim it as our rightful place and to condescend to those who sit down beside us? What right have we to this table, this feast, and this country? Those of us non-Indigenous people living in post-colonial settler societies have very little right. But we may perhaps earn a right to feel proud of, and a part of, our home country if we have contributed constructively to its culture, its politics, and its traditions of openness and enfranchisement; if, in short, we are engaged in supporting a political community that does not oppress its own or others, and that "sees itself in solidarity with the oppressed, wherever they are" (Arendt again, in her book *The Origins of Totalitarianism*).

If we live in such a community we may feel proud, but we are unlikely to condescend to the refugees who turn to us for assistance. We will see them instead as human beings who have known oppression and who suffer the hardships of exile, but who embody the hope of a world in which the agency of every human being is recognised and honoured.

"We Refugees" focuses on the plight of Jewish exiles who had left their "relatives in Polish ghettos" and whose "best friends [had] been killed in concentration camps." In many respects, Arendt's subjects were unlike other refugees. As she describes it, the Jewish people in Europe had a distinctive history and culture, and even the desire shown by many to assimilate in the host countries to which they fled was idiomatic, revealing characteristics forged through their long history as an outsider people. But despite the distinctiveness of the Jewish experience, the events of WWII were to prove that it was also representative, for "the outlawing of the Jewish people in Europe [was] followed closely by the outlawing" of many other peoples, including the Slavic, Roma, and Polish. Moreover, people were not targeted solely on the basis of their race or religion, but also because of their anti-fascist political commitments, or their profession, or sexuality, or because they were destitute.

What the experience of the WWII refugees demonstrates is that the tragedy of exile and loss of home can happen to anyone. What Arendt's analysis suggests is that whether we are refuges or citizens of countries where people seek refuge, each of us has agency and a responsibility to act. It is for these reasons that the title *We Refugees* was chosen for this book. Rather than a vision of crisis, what readers will find in the poems, stories, and personal reflections that follow are moving accounts of individual suffering and fortitude; demonstrations of the great willingness shared by many to bridge cultural divides and offer hope and healing; and celebrations of the courage of people who have been forced to leave their homes and seek new ones. It is perhaps notable that only one of the contributors is herself a refugee. The other contributors write from a variety of experiences: working with refugees; knowing the loss and suffering of family members who are refugees; or simply empathising with the refugee experience. The book's title is apposite as a reminder that each of us is only ever a step or two removed from the experience of exile. Especially in today's globalised world, exile implicates and potentially affects us all.

᠀

I am deeply grateful to the authors for their contributions; and to artist Alex Johnson, and Virginia Ryan and the Make Art Not Walls/Italia Collective for permission to reproduce the painting used on our cover. Thank you as well to Julian Burnside for his tireless advocacy work over many years, and for his support of this project.

Finally, big thank yous to my dear friends Leonie Martino—for her constant generosity and excellent suggestions for improvements to this essay; and Kirsty Anantharajah—for her thoughts on a couple of the contributions in this book and most of all, for her irrepressible enthusiasm and steady encouragement.

The work of everyone involved has been donated in order to support the Asylum Seeker Resource Centre (ASRC) in Melbourne, Australia. All proceeds from book sales will go to the ASRC to assist in its mission supporting and empowering asylum seekers.

Emma Larking is a social and legal researcher based in Melbourne, Australia. She is author of *Refugees and the Myth of Human Rights: Life Outside the Pale of the Law* (Ashgate 2014/Routledge, 2017), and co-editor with Hilary Charlesworth of *Human Rights and the Universal Periodic Review* (Cambridge University Press, 2014). Her disciplinary backgrounds are in literature, law, political theory, and applied philosophy. She has published widely on the concept and status of human rights, and on refugees and people movements.

Dusk

Robert Gamble

Dayheat leaves the earth
all of sudden, a silent shout.

Ay! how the known world rotates,
mesquite shadows lengthening
to stretch a bleached desert floor.

Mourning doves take up their
mourning.

First stars.

Down-canyon, migrants emerge
from crevasses
carrying jugs marked
with the Sacred Heart
and ¡*Vaya con Dios!*

They point their feet

across the threshold

of the unimaginable,

as darkness

scrubs the rockfaces of all

traces of afterglow.

৯

Robbie Gamble works as a nurse practitioner caring for homeless people in Boston. He spends time every summer on the Arizona/Mexico border, providing medical and material support to migrants who are passing through a remote and dangerous section of the Sonoran Desert. His poems and essays have appeared in *Scoundrel Time*, *Writers Resist*, *Solstice*, *Poet Lore*, and *Carve*, among others.

SHEM[1]

Nina Foushee

The summer after my first year in college, I worked in Nogales, in Sonora, Mexico as an intern for a community foundation. I was housesitting in Rio Rico, Arizona, a twenty minute
drive from the border. Though I had no real job, I spent each
weekday with migrants. Most days, I went to English and
nutrition classes taught by other volunteers, and spent time at
the *comedor*, a day shelter a few paces from the border wall. In
the evenings, I drove home, parked in the remote-controlled
garage, and read my paperback copy of *Anna Karenina* with a
cup of boxed wine on the front porch.

My car radio didn't work. On the way to Sonora I'd listen to
Silvio Rodríguez, the only music on my computer. My laptop
remained perched on the passenger seat, a kind of compan-
ion with whom I could only have one conversation. I'd turn
Silvio up loud as I could, playing Canción de Navidad for
the saguaros. *Por eso canto a quien no escucha...,/ al que su cotidiana
lucha/ me da razones para amarle/ a aquel que nadie le cantó.*[2]

I could make sense of nothing that summer: my theme

---

[1] 'Shem' is the eldest son of Noah in the Hebrew Bible – the Hebrew
word 'shem' is most often translated as 'name'.
[2] 'That is why I sing to the one who doesn't listen...,/to the one
whose/daily struggle/gives me reasons to love him/to the person
who nobody sings to.'

song for the three months was about Christmas. After a few weeks of crossing to Sonora every day, Border Patrol agents started to recognize me. The camaraderie we had, white person to white person, was nauseating. One time, a younger officer took my passport and winked: "Old enough to drink here!" My mouth opened into a smile I did not feel. A part of me hated that officer.

Another time in the border line, a Mexican man behind me asked if I was a missionary. My long skirt, pale skin, and tote bag suggested some need to convey the quiet of my life twenty minutes north of where we stood together. I told him I wasn't, but I felt exposed. Did he know how much I wanted to have complete faith in something, something for which I could choose to be a conduit? The summer was a series of crossings: the movement made me feel that I knew myself, and the place on each side of the line, less and less.

At the door to the *comedor*, the priests in charge checked for government papers which served as proof of deportation. Most people came in broken, sunburned, and unsteady on their feet. When I wanted to hold people, to say the right words, I directed them to the right sized pair of socks. Sometimes, I sat after the meal and listened to people tell stories of separation: from sisters, parents, country.

After a month or so of going back and forth between Rio Rico and Nogales, I drove home to Tucson to attend the Hebrew naming ceremony for the daughter of a close family friend. Around thirty people came to the Jewish history museum for the ceremony. We picked at cheese, fruit, and wine and settled into wooden chairs. We were watched by Jewish settlers in Arizona from the 1800s: mannequins in glass cases with fixed stares. It was the only time that summer that I dressed up and combed my hair. The sun drifted down, refracted in motes of dust, as Rabbi Linda spoke about how each child embodies all of creation. She started with the idea that in Genesis, God made light first. She noted that within each child lies the ability to bring more light into the world. Djuna, a delightful little creature in purple dress and frilled socks, gurgled. When we'd reached the seventh day of creation, Djuna stuck her hand in the goblet of wine. Everyone around me was clapping, and I felt myself putting my hands together, an act that contained very little of what I felt.

My mind went to two children at the *comedor*, two children who had been deported trying to cross the desert in the middle of July. Together we sang for Djuna, a being and a world complete. The rabbi began: *hava nagila, hava nagila, hava*—Hebrew for "let us rejoice." I could not get out the first word. Sitting in my wooden chair, brushed by the wind of so many voices, I felt that I was with the girl and her little brother, who had possessed a cheerfulness I could not place. Those children had passed through my life, and, unlike Djuna, would never appear as a beaming picture on my refrigerator. *Hava nagila, havaaaa.* I remember when someone brought bubbles to the *comedor*, how this brother and sister had chased each other with the wands. Each child, a world: transparent and whole. The song ended and I was left knowing I would never see that pair again. My head was in the next verse in Psalm 124, the one that isn't in the song: "please ADONAI! Save us! Please, ADONAI! Rescue us!" The children I remember, the brother and sister, were some of the lucky ones: they were able to cross with shoes. Their 18 year old aunt had been the one responsible for escorting them. They had already been deported twice. Djuna's world could never intersect with the ones that the children at the *comedor* would encounter. I could not sing.

Mary Oliver's "Wild Geese" looped through my mind: *You do not have to be good./ You do not have to walk on your knees/ for a hundred miles through the desert, repenting.* The words constricted the rest of my thoughts. People stood to leave and Djuna's paediatrician talked to me about Stanford, the "'ole Cardinal red." I tried to seem as though I hadn't been crying. When I was younger, before I had accepted that I wasn't Jewish, I wanted to be a rabbi. I wanted to answer the questions which could never be stories with stories. There was no story to explain the desert I now felt, the one between the child being named and the ones whose futures seemed un-nameable.

A few weeks later, I went to another naming ceremony of sorts: a border conference in El Paso that billed itself as an attempt to "reframe the narrative of the border." A few women from a Texas immigration non-profit gave a presentation about migrant deaths. They handed each attendee a card with a picture of a middle-school aged girl on it. The back of the card gave a brief story of her attempt to cross the border. Beneath the story was the date at which she was found in the desert, dead from dehydration. It was the kind of thing one would get as a laminated prayer for a saint at a church gift shop. The women gave us a 3x5 of a girl's life. She still lives in my wallet, but her face is bent, having been folded for some time around my credit card and driver's license.

My mom sent me updates on the baby Djuna: a giggle, a word, a new favorite food. The next few weeks in Rio Rico,

I did everything except sit with what I had seen. I woke up early each morning to make a cup of coffee and watch the sun Windex the day's surface bright and flat. A few times, I bought eggs from the feed store in an adjacent town, and I'd cook one or two in lots of butter. I picked the figs before the bugs came and waited for sales on produce at the town's one grocery store. Halfway through *Anna Karenina*, I worked up the courage to kill a scorpion on the shower wall. I bought more boxed wine with my sister's ID, thinking: *so this is how alcoholism starts.* James Brown played on Pandora while I watered houseplants and made the bed. I made myself comfortable: I subscribed to Netflix.

I wanted to drive the dirt roads around Rio Rico once before returning home permanently. People in the town told me to drive slowly, saying, "If you kill a cow around here, you pay by the pound." At ten miles an hour, I could actually see all the dust and empty space. Who is expected to pay for the human bodies that turn up in the desert? I got onto the freeway, a way of running from the question. Outside the car window, a monsoon beat the sky a deep purple, making everything smell of creosote.

Nina Foushee is a writer, essay tutor, and communications manager who loves absurdist comedy. Though she lives in San Francisco, she has an abiding love for the Sonoran Desert where she was raised. She likes to explore how stories inform our moral life.

LAYA &ASEEL

Loretta Oleck

Laya and Aseel, thirteen years old,
need to be babied, but it is too late
for babying.

Mothers fold sorrows like laundry.

The girls suck stones, imagining
they are peppermint candies.

They steal crayons, plastic beads,
and bits of string.

They slap the cheeks of children,
then cry, pretending they were struck first.

Mothers fold sorrows like laundry.

In the evenings, Laya and Aseel
wedge their sleepy siblings
into wobbly strollers, then push them
round the tents, the distribution center,
and the latrines.

Their dark eyes remain focused
on this journey of circles,
on this labyrinth
with no beginning, and no end.

Mothers hang sweaters and slacks
from tangled webs of clothing lines.

Stolen trinkets —
stubs of crayons, random beads, bits
of string, an occasional cat-eyed marble
tumble from pockets like gems.

આ

Loretta Oleck, 2016 Pushcart Poetry Prize nominee, is the author of two poetry collections, *Songs from the Black Hole* (Finishing Line Press), and *Persephone Dreaming of Cherries* (Hurricane Press). Her poetry and photography have been published in *The Stockholm Review of Literature*, *The Adirondack Review*, *The Missing Slate*, *Obsidian Literature*, *Black Lawrence Press*, *So to Speak: Feminist Journal of Language and Art*, *Feminist Studies*, *Picayune Magazine*, *Poetica Literary Magazine*, *WordRiot*, among numerous others. Her poetry was filmed for the Public Poetry Series, included in *Storm Cycle's Best of 2013 Anthology*, and has been performed at dozens of venues. She received an MA in Creative Writing from New York University and an MSW in Social Work from Fordham University. In 2016, Loretta volunteered through Lighthouse Relief at a camp for Syrian refugees—Ritsona Refugee Camp—in Ritsona, Greece. She worked mostly with the children meeting their unique psychological and social needs through supportive activities, creative expression, and play.

LETTER FROM SYRIA

Enesa Mahmić

My friend,
One completely plain morning
While drinking tea and carelessly reading the newspaper
The dogs of war knocked on my door

From this moment on there are no newspapers
No bread, no tea on my desk anymore
The laughter of my children is gone

Now
In the middle of the chaos we are constantly trying to find
New survival tactics

Here—
  Death steadily increases
There—
  Heartless politicians
  And academics bury their heads in the sand.

∾

Enesa Mahmić is an Bosnian travel writer, poetess, and feminist. She is a member of PEN Center. Her travel stories and poetry have appeared in many journals including *Words and Worlds Magazine, Dubai Poetics, Balkan Literary Herald*, and *Eckermann*. Her work has also appeared in anthologies such as *Social Justice and Intersectional Feminism* (University of Victoria, Canada), *Spread poetry, not fear* (Slovenia), *QUEEN Global voices of 21th century female Poets* (India), *Le Voci della poesia; Imagine & Poesia* (Italy), *Writing Politics and Knowledge Production* (Zimbabwe), *Wood poets* (Croatia), *World for peace* (World Institute for Peace, Nigeria), and more. She is the recipient of the following awards for literature: Ratković's Evenings of Poetry 2016, gold medal for best immigrant poetry for "Neighbour of your shore 2017," and the Aladin Lukač Award 2016 for best debut book.

My Name is Monica Akur

Akuol Garang

I began to think that God really hated me. I started questioning my faith!

My name is Monica Akur. I was once a Christian.

1989

My husband had just returned, wounded, from the war. He was a child soldier. I vividly remember people running, children screaming, and my mother-in-law shouting at me: "Run my daughter, run my daughter, they are here, the soldiers are here." The war had finally reached our village in Sudan. I could hear the sound of tanks and soldiers attacking. Within minutes, houses were burning. There was smoke clouding the air, making it difficult to see. I ran, following the crowd as I watched the fire ravage and burn our entire beloved home.

With nowhere to go, my husband and I, his ten-year-old nephew and eight-year-old niece, fled toward Ethiopia. I became the children's mother as we walked for months trying to reach Ethiopia. Sometimes we stayed in large fields where aid workers would set up camp.

1990

After months of walking, we eventually made it to a place

called Panyido refugee camp in Ethiopia. We lived in the camp in Panyido for a year. There, I gave birth to my first born—a boy—but with no proper medical treatment and healthcare services in the camp, my son caught a simple flu. It took his life. His name was Deng.

I started questioning my faith; "Why lord, why are you doing this to me? First my village and now my child." I wanted to give up on life. I had no more hope left in me. I was a teenager, I had just lost my first child, and I was now caring for my husband, nephew, and niece in a foreign land. I thought things couldn't get worse, but they did.

1991

Ethiopia was at war. Our camp was attacked by rebels following the overthrow of the Mengistu regime, and this forced us to begin another journey to a new camp. My life became a life of travelling from one camp to another.

Again, we spent months walking, this time trying to make our way back to Sudan. I was five months pregnant with my second child. We had no choice but to flee: it was either die or run and hope for the best. Thousands of people died; some drowned trying to swim through the river back to Sudan. I was lucky.

I walked to the point where I became extremely tired. The baby started moving; it felt as if I was going into labour at five months—surely that could not be right? Fear consumed me, my body became weak and still. Was I losing my baby? I could no longer move. I told my husband to stop walking: "I can't do this anymore, we have to stop! I think the baby is coming? Can we stop?" I remember mumbling these exact words to my husband as we stopped in the middle of nowhere on the side of a dirt road, with no food, no water, and no shelter. I was seventeen years old and five months pregnant with my second child.

My husband stopped, he put a small blanket on the side of the dirt road and we slept there. I no longer worried whether a person would come out of the bush in the middle of the night and kill me, nor that hyenas could take my life. I remember seeing other refugees walking by, holding their children's hands. No one stopped to help. They had been through so much; many had lost their own children and members of their families—they had their own pain to deal with. My condition was nothing special, I was just another statistic.

In the morning the baby had calmed down, so we decided to resume the journey. I began walking again and eventually we found another refugee camp on the border of Ethiopia and Sudan. We stayed in a place called Pochalla until my daughter was born.

It was the rainy season, there were no dry surfaces. It was midnight and my husband struggled to find a surface that I could lie on as I began going into labour. We had no electricity, no midwife, no medical supplies. We struggled through the dark and I lay down on grass that felt wet and greasy, but I did not care. My baby was coming and that was all that mattered.

I started praying to the God I had stopped believing in, to bless me with the safe delivery of my daughter. He listened. My daughter was born, though I was not able to see her face until the morning. I held her close to my chest. I hugged her and listened to her cries and her beautiful small heartbeat. On the morning of August 13, 1991, I finally laid eyes on her. It was magic. I did not want to worry about the fact that there was no food or baby formula: at that moment in time I was blessed. My daughter's name is Akuol.

Late 1991

In the camps, the United Nations High Commissioner for Refugees provided us with only maize flour; no oil or salt. I tried to use what we had to survive. I lived on this maize straight after giving birth. With nothing else mixed with it, I became quite ill. For two months I was sick. I thought I was going to die. I believe the strength of my daughter is what kept me alive. I did not want to die and leave my daughter in a world with no mother. The world had already tested me. Life had become a matter of survival: I had survived until then. I would not leave my daughter. I would survive.

1992

"Hush my child, do not make any noise, the bad people will hear us!" My daughter kept crying. She was scared of the dark and confused. My husband had dug a hole where we hid, hoping and praying that the soldiers would not find us. It was six months after the birth of my daughter, and Pochalla was under attack.

We had to flee yet again, this time to Kapoeta, on the Kenyan border, but things were worse there. One of my relatives, a captain at the time, was killed. We were even more scared, so we started moving again. It took three days to make it to the next camp, Lokichoggio, in northern Kenya, but even there our troubles were not over. I became a victim of repeat attacks, not by the soldiers, but this time by the local tribes of that region. We fled again, eventually making it to our last camp, Kakuma refugee camp.

Kakuma

Kakuma is the Swahili word for *nowhere*. I literally felt like I was nowhere. This camp was different to many of the camps I had been to previously. The other camps were temporary; in them we had no sense of identity or belonging. But Kakuma, even though it was a nowhere place, also became our place: it was established in 1992 for Sudanese refugees by the United Nations High Commissioner for Refugees. In the years that followed it expanded to host refugees from many different countries. New arrivals are allocated to different sections of the camp, in "groups," and given Identity cards. We lived in group 48. I remember arriving and being welcomed by dust storms. It was always hot and humid. I wondered how I would survive.

1993

My third child was born in 1993. His name is Garang. A year had passed in Kakuma and I had survived. There was no more running: Kakuma had indeed become our home. It would be home for ten years.

1996

In 1996, I gave birth to my fourth child. Her name is Akeer. With nowhere to go, I wanted to use the few resources we had and to provide a better life for my children. I started making homemade beer and sold it in the local street market. My business soon picked up and I had regular customers. With the money I made, I bought clothes and shoes for my children. Occasionally, my children were able to have sugar in their porridge. When things were really good, they had beef in their stew.

I became a preschool teacher. As a teacher, I discovered the importance of education for my children. This became the driving force for me. I worked hard and hoped for a better future for my children.

2001

In October 2001, God answered my prayers. I was granted a permanent humanitarian visa to a country called Australia. It had been ten long years in the Kakuma refugee camp, but my family and I would now be free: free from fear and oppression. Free to plan our future.

In Australia, I hoped for a better life.

My name is Monica Akur and I am a Christian.

Akuol Garang and her family fled from war in Sudan when she was a child and spent ten years in a refugee camp in Kenya before migrating to Australia in 2001. "My Name is Monica Akur" is a story about her mother's strength and resilience. Despite hardships and trauma, Monica Akur's story also highlights the resilience of the refugee women of Sudan, who all share similar journeys and stories to Akur; stories that have not been told; important stories that need to be heard.

Akuol is a speaker and a storyteller, and has had her work featured by the broadcaster SBS, and in ANZ Bluenotes and Voices for Freedom. She is studying a Masters of Human Rights Law at Monash University. Akuol is a registered Migration Agent, working and volunteering to support migrants and refugees in Australia. She is passionate about building and mobilizing communities, and advocating for the rights of refugees and people seeking asylum. She uses her lived experiences to highlight the positive contributions that people from refugee backgrounds bring to the Australian community.

WHAT THE TÍOS SAY

Robert Gamble

Ay, Chema,
those *coyotes*, they promised you
this wouldn't be so hard, didn't they?
Un día caminando, just a day's walk
from the border to the highway
and the van to carry you on to Phoenix.
Muchacho, they took all your money,
said *¡Andale!* come quickly now,
follow us. *Y tu sabes*, understand now,
we all know what happens next.

On your second day of walking
a helicopter drops from the sky,
buzzes your group, and in the blinding
dust and noise, *La Migra*,
those green-clad men on ATVs
zoom in, they scatter you
and hunt down stragglers.
You flatten, lizard-like
behind some boulders
and wait for dark, all alone.

Then it's day again, and canyons' walls
curve and twist like red rock curtains
hiding the distant mountains
they said you should aim for.
This sun, it just hangs over you,
refuses to blink or give direction.
Chema, *mi hijo*, what will become of you,
wandering and wandering, and this thirst
that tries to pull your throat apart?

Maybe you will find a cattle trough
thick with scum, and you will drink
then vomit all that is left in you.
Perhaps you will come across a cache
left by Samaritans: a jug of pure water,
a can of beans to sustain you moving on.
Perhaps La Migra slashed the jug,
its brittle gallon shell mocks you in the dust.

Or there will be nothing to find, nothing at all,
and your weakened circles will wind down.
Or else another patrol will grab you anyway,
zip-tie you up, fling you like roadkill
back over the border, broke and thirsty
to start over.

❧

REFUGEES AND IMMIGRANTS

Steven Jakobi

Like the millions before you,
caught in dark corners of history,
born in the wrong place, at the wrong time,
you came to these shores
wanting freedom and prosperity.

Sons of Hibernia,
Daughters of Palermo,
Diaspora of Jews,
Refugees of Saigon,
you came to these shores
wanting freedom and prosperity.

Migrants escaping tyrants,
refugees of war, famine,
poverty and serfdom,
you came to the Promised Land,
(whose streets, you thought,
were paved with gold),
wanting freedom and prosperity.

Did you ask the Senecas, the Lakotas,
the Apaches, the Sioux, the Mikmaq,
if you were welcome, if you were
wanted, if you were legal,
when you came to these shores
seeking freedom and prosperity?

Have you forgotten your past?
Your ancestors' history?
How can you gaze at Lady Liberty
in the harbor and
deny suffering people their
chance of freedom and prosperity?

You want to build walls,
you want to send armies,
shamelessly you follow charlatans,
to keep out people who are just like you were
when you came to these shores
wanting freedom and prosperity.

Steven Jakobi is a retired college biology professor. He is
the author of two books of very short essays on the lessons
we can learn from nature. He also writes short fiction and
poetry. A native of Hungary, Jakobi and his wife live in rural
Allegany County, New York, with three dogs, two cats, and
many chickens.

ON BELONGING

Kirsty Anantharajah

There are days in this country when you wonder
what your role in this country is and your place in it.
How precisely are you going to reconcile yourself
to your situation here and how you are [sic] going
to communicate to the…white majority that you are
here? I am terrified at the moral apathy, the death of
the heart, which is happening in my country. These
people deluded themselves for so long that they really don't think I'm human.

- James Baldwin

Reading Baldwin's reflection on life and identity as a black
man in 1960s America was one of the first times that I realised that my own relationship with and identity in my country
are complex. I read these words long after my secondary education, during which I had spent years studying only white
authors. Finding Baldwin, I was struck by the fact that someone in a vastly different situation to my own understood my
experience. It appeared that this eternal crisis of identity in
my gut had been known before me and indeed had a name.

Baldwin's reflections drove my quest to consider my own
identity. Black culture and black movements have long been

appropriated desperately by brown kids in white countries, and this is not right. This appropriation occurs for a fundamentally different reason than appropriation by white Americans of black communities, as articulated by Ta-Nehisi Coates: "When you're white in this country, you're taught that everything belongs to you." We cling to black culture not because we have been raised to entitlement over spaces and cultures; rather because, for many of us, we have not had a secure cultural space to call our own. For many of us second generation migrants and refugees, black stories and resistance are far more resonant than the white majoritarian narratives dominating institutions, reading lists, and popular culture. For many of us, our encounter with these stories and resistance is the first time we feel the world reflect back an existence resembling our own.

This reliance on black culture to affirm our non-white identity comes also from an absence. Comparatively little has been said or written or debated by brown people in public spaces about our distinct identities in our host countries. Such debate has not been welcomed in contexts that prefer we focus our energies on assimilation. This hopefully explains why the genius of black writers like Baldwin and Coates are, perhaps incongruously, my grappling hooks in this essay that attempts to make sense of a conflicted identity: a Tamil member of the Australian public.

The Tamil Australian story

Sri Lankan Tamils are one of the largest groups of asylum seekers and refugees in Australia. Recent interactions between the Australian state and Sri Lankan asylum seekers have been fraught. This is evidenced by odious government policies—policies dictating the disruption of desperate journeys; that require the imprisonment of those who have committed no crime; that dehumanise and exclude. In some iterations these policies have applied only to Sri Lankan Tamils.[1] It is also evidenced by lives, and their destruction. Leo Seemampilai, a twenty-nine-year-old Tamil refugee who arrived in Darwin in 2013 by boat from Indonesia, was living and working in Geelong, Victoria on a temporary visa. He self-immolated in 2014, unable to bear the stress of living constantly in limbo—purgatory Australian style. 'Rajah,' another Tamil man, was deported to Sri Lanka in 2018 without his case for asylum being considered; credible sources warned Australia that he was in danger of being detained and tortured on his return. Nadesalingam and Priya, and their Australian born daughters, aged seven months and two and a half years, were removed from their beds and their home in Biloela, Queensland by Australian Border Force officials in a dawn raid on 5 March, 2018. The family had been in Australia for four years, but their temporary protection visas had expired the day before. The family is currently in detention, and confronting the prospect of deportation, and also in danger of being separated indefinitely.[2]

---

[1] Since 2012, the claims of Sri Lankan asylum seekers have been determined in accordance with an 'enhanced screening' process. The decision-making criteria and reasons for a screening decision are not provided, creating a procedure without transparency or accountability. At its inception, enhanced screening was used exclusively to assess the protection claims of Sri Lankan asylum seekers.

[2] As of June 2018. An injunction prevents Priya and her eldest daughter being deported in the short term.

Insecurity and loss seems to have followed our community from our motherland. In Sri Lanka, villages whose names we grew up knowing as well as our own no longer exist in the same way; no longer hubs of community life, they are flooded with soldiers and riddled with land mines. My mother left in 1983, in Black July, at the start of the civil war. Since then, as the war raged, the Tamil community has been killed, disappeared, and violated; in 2009, the last stages of the war saw the most profound loss of life. We use the word genocide. The post-war period presented new and enduring horrors for Tamils, which is why so many Tamil people have risked the journey to Australia.

The knowledge that we were hated, reviled, and threatened in Sri Lanka was a knowledge I had from birth. This knowledge of oppression in Sri Lanka is a part of Tamil identity. I accepted it proudly, as a legacy from my ancestors and community that survived it. The knowledge that persecuted Tamils are no longer welcome in Australia—a realisation that has grown stronger with every returned boat—has forced me to grapple with questions of my own identity as an Australian citizen and a proud Tamil woman.

Conflict of identities

While for many years my two identities coexisted relatively peacefully within me, since 2001, the Australian Government's treatment of asylum seekers has brought about an irreconcilable conflict. In wooing the public vote, successive Governments have colluded in oppressing the most vulnerable members of my community. How can I be a member of the public who feels exhilarated at political calls to "stop the boats"?

When one of the Aunties rings around our houses, collecting money to send the body of a Tamil asylum seeker back to his mother in Sri Lanka, I know I cannot be. When a man who survived the horrors of the Sri Lankan civil war loses hope on our shores, I know I cannot be. Working in a refugee legal clinic in Western Sydney, when I read near identical protection visa refusal decisions to six Tamil clients in a row—decisions that seek to gaslight our community and deny Tamil suffering—I know where I stand. When a man is deported to Sri Lanka without any pretence of due process, and I fear what horror awaits him at Bandaranaiyake airport, I know that my identities no longer coexist peacefully.

The lives of Tamil refugees and asylum seekers in Australia have altered my perception of my country, and more specifically, my place within it. My own privileged position, and right to belonging and safety, which is elevated in the public hierarchy over other members of my community who have arrived in recent years seeking refuge, somehow feels less assured. The strange territory that separates me from the vilified members of my community who are expelled or imprisoned in camps run by Australia on Manus Island and Nauru are built on rather nebulous distinctions. Firstly, the temporal distinction that allowed my family to come legally and relatively smoothly to Australia in the 1980s. We came on a lucky tide. Secondly, I was born here, although this achievement has offered little to Priya's daughters, currently spending what should be precious moments of their childhood in immigration detention. The last factor accounts for most of what sense of security is left to me: I have successfully assimilated. I barely speak Tamil, most of my friends are white, and my English is communicated with a strong Australian accent.

Assimilation is Australia's political soma, feeding us non-white Australians the myth of belonging. It is designed to make me forget that beyond being Australian I am also Tamil, and it is my community that my beloved country has chosen to persecute.

Conditional belonging

Our belonging in Australia is, and has long been, conditional. For me, for most of my life, I accepted these conditions blindly and wholeheartedly. And these conditions dug out deep and dry gullies in my identity. I lost my mother tongue. My social circles discuss their yoga retreats to "peaceful" Sri Lanka, which is a world apart from my community's experience of flight and exile. My belonging is conditioned on my assimilation: beyond linguistic and cultural assimilation, there is a darker, even more troubling form of assimilation that is required of my community. We never speak of it, but it's there. Our belonging is conditioned on our ability to assimilate into the majoritarian ideology, we are required to internalise the structural racism to which we are subjected.

> As people of color are victimized by racism, we internalize it. That is, we develop ideas, beliefs, actions and behaviors that support or collude with racism. This internalized racism has its own systemic reality and its own negative consequences in the lives and communities of people of color. More than just a consequence of racism, then, internalized racism is a systemic oppression in reaction to racism that has a

life of its own. In other words, just as there is a system in place that reinforces the power and expands the privilege of white people, there is a system in place that actively discourages and undermines the power of people and communities of color and mires us in our own oppression. Individuals, institutions and communities of color are often unconsciously and habitually rewarded for supporting white privilege and power and punished and excluded when we do not. This system of oppression often coerces us to let go of or compromise our own better judgment, thus diminishing everyone as the diversity of human experience and wisdom is excluded.

- Donna Bivins

While there is disagreement about the extent of support or acquiescence, Australia's "ethnic" voters do not seem to be particularly averse to draconian and cruel asylum seeker policies. Why do those of us with lived and personal experience of displacement and racism, and with the power of the vote, not represent a challenge to political platforms like "Stop the Boats"? Because we are, as Bivins articulates, rewarded for supporting white privilege: we are rewarded with belonging, these are the motions of assimilation. And indeed it is a matter of race. Australia's asylum seeker policies are supremely racist, and their architects and advocates do little to hide it. As the plight of the Rohingya in Myanmar and in refugee camps in Bangladesh worsens—a crisis in our region involving suffering on a tremendous scale—Australia refuses special concessions to displaced members of this community.

Our Minister for Home Affairs has, however, publically called for special conditions to be applied to the "persecuted" class of white South African farmers in order to allow them to immigrate more easily.

Belonging in the diaspora

The Sri Lanka of the diaspora, of the second generation, is not the same Sri Lanka that exists in flesh and blood and land. My Sri Lanka is woven from the sepia tinted stories of our parents and grandparents of the tea estates, the jungle and the terraces of Colombo. Here belonging was complete: our stories were often sanitized from their context of ethnic divides, of postcolonial unravelling, of a seething hatred. Our Sri Lanka is both the memory of a mother, and a constant spectre of loss. And our relationship with it will never be simple, it will never be free of contradictions. We want nothing more than to return, yet we never go a day without thanking God that we got out.

I have returned twice. Once as a child when my mother brought my sister and I back because we begged her to show us where we came from. I did not know at the time, but her constantly round eyes, her shaking hands, her clenching fists betrayed the fact that all she wanted to do was forget—forget where she came from and why she left.

The next time I returned I was eighteen. I flew into Colombo, went as far north as I could, and worked in a vocational camp for girls and women on the outskirts of the jungle. Here they shared with me the horrors of the war that they were surviving. They told me that most of their families were recently murdered, their villages burnt. They drew pictures of their journeys, punctuated by shelling. In that jungle we would play cricket, make lamb curry, and we would laugh together. When I dropped them back off at one of Sri Lanka's notorious IDP camps, we cried together. It was, and probably will always be, one of the worst and hardest moments of my life.

This was my first taste of being a "real" Tamil, the kind that did not get out. The kind who lost their homeland not through migration, but through genocide, the kind who lost their families, and their agency, and often their bodies in camps, and then in militarised zones masquerading as villages.

On this trip a car bomb exploded down the street. Days later, a member of the army held a gun in my face at a checkpoint I had to cross to get to work. The power and recklessness in his face only made sense to me later, when I joined a team of Sri Lankan women investigating sexual violence perpetrated by the military against Tamil women during the conflict. Even though his superior officer slapped his gun away, I inherited a fear of checkpoints that day, the same that drew blood from my mother's knuckles when our car would pass them on the streets of Colombo years before.

My few lived experiences of Sri Lanka influence my connection to this country far less than the experiences of my ancestors. The guns in my family stories were not wielded by soldiers but by my Appa, breaking up a family trip to our ancestral home to hunt fowls in the jungle. They would stop the car, Appa would procure the bird and Ammama would make the best jungle fowl curry the world had ever seen. Stories of road trips were not ones characterised by military checkpoints or the guerrilla tactics of the Tigers, but rather laughingly delivered narratives of having to fit twelve cousins into the back seat on the way up North.

The North, Jaffna, is our Tamil heartland and the home of my ancestors. It is a place I have never been to but its villages are carved in my heart. Our maternal home, the home of my grandmother's mother, is located in the North near the village of Thellipilai. This place, more than any other, characterizes my longing. Our maternal clan was named the "brave knives" and our home was called Veramanai, "the home of the brave."

The story of the diaspora is also often the story of exile: this is particularly true for those of us who fall into the maligned categories of writers, journalists, or human rights defenders. It is possible I may never return again; may never see, never arrive, at our Veramanai. When I realised this, it was hard to be brave. For days, I would use Google maps to walk around Thellipalai, trying to engineer the kind of homecoming my feet might never have.

The Tamil inheritance is something I had to face in that moment—including the privilege of my own particular inheritance. The diaspora, we who left before the final years of the war, those of us who boast citizenship and permanent residency in other countries, are indeed lucky. We are the hope in the hearts of those who make the journey across the seas in order to have a semblance of what we represent: Tamil safety; Tamil lives free from the constant threat of violence; an escape from the long shadow cast by genocide of Tamil peoples.

The Sri Lanka my mother ran from was a much less frightening place than it grew to be, and that it still is. The riots that burned our family home and business to the ground and led

40

to the slaughter of our friends and community spurred our migration. Our conflict experience ended at what was just the beginning for most Tamils. From Black July, the violence in Sri Lanka worsened, became less *ad hoc* and more institutionalised. The deepest of my grandfather's fears of Tamil suffering became flesh and blood, and materialised in Sri Lanka's black torture sites, in its practice of "white vanning," in its "final offensive."

I do not know the country from where these thousands of Tamil men and women flee. It is a terrible knowledge that those who make the journey carry in their hearts and that fuels their boats. When I reflect on these maritime journeys, I need to think that something more than this trauma motivates the quest for safe lands—I like to imagine my people travelling, as my mother did, with a little hope in their hearts. But what happens to these hopes, as insubstantial and perhaps imaginary as they might be, when these journeys are halted by the force of Australia's navy and border patrols (as has been the reality for over 1,100 Tamils) and when Australia—the hoped for protector—delivers them back into the hands of Ravana?[3]

The power of complex identities

There is a German community: both sides of Berlin, Bavaria and Yorkville. There is an Italian community: Rome, Naples, the Bank of the Holy Ghost and Mulberry Street. And there is a Jewish community, stretching from Jerusalem to California to New

---

[3] Ravana is the mythical demon king of Lanka in the Hindu epic the *Ramayana*.

York. There are English communities. There are French communities. There are Swiss consortiums. There are Poles …

It bears terrifying witness to what happened to everyone who got here, and paid the price of the ticket. The price was to become "white." No one was white before he/she came to America. It took generations, and a vast amount of coercion, before this became a white country.

- Baldwin

Complex identities are not just the inheritance of people of colour. The Australian State is young: in this country, all but Aboriginal Australians are migrants and its colonisers were "boat people." Perhaps it is these complex identities that are the answer to more humane and empathetic treatment of refugees in our nation. In 1984, Baldwin penned a very powerful essay for *Essence* magazine titled, "On being white…and other lies." Here he shows that white people too have accepted certain conditions, have lost cultural heritages, and have assimilated. Complex ethnic identities like Latvian-Greek-Australian are traded for the privilege of being a "white Australian." Yet the reward for white assimilation is not simply belonging—it is power.

Superficially at least, my uncle Stevie is a white Australian. When the topic of asylum seeker policy comes up though, Stevie is a Latvian-Greek-Australian. He cannot broach the conversation without emotion: his own mother, a holocaust survivor, was orphaned as an infant at the conclusion of WWII. In the care of a loving aunt, she made the difficult journey through Europe as a refugee. Stevie sees the global flows of asylum seekers not as threats to our shores, but as families without the privilege of options, running for their lives. My white (Latvian-Greek-Australian) uncle will take this issue to the polling booth.

So what if people of colour, and people who have the option of being "white," do not accept the Australian conditions —what if we refuse to assimilate? We may lose a belonging predicated on the denial of our identities, and lose a power derived from the subjugation of others. It's possible, though, that we might also gain more humane and less racist refugee and asylum seeker policies.

Conclusion

> I know how you watch as you grow older, the corpses of your brothers and your sisters pile up around you. Not as a result of anything they have done, they were too young to have done anything. But what one does realize is that when you try to stand up and look the world in the face as if you had a right to be here, you have attacked the entire power structure of the western world.
>
> - Baldwin

The more I grapple with my identity, the less I am able to acquiesce to the conditions now attached to belonging in Australia. I want to be a citizen of a country that I can bring my whole self to: an Australia that grows richer by including my Tamil heritage in its social fabric. An Australia that does not seek to eradicate my history. Most importantly, an Australia where my belonging does not rest on complicity in the denial, exclusion, and suffering of my people.

჻

Kirsty Anantharajah—proud Tamil woman and member of the Sri Lankan diaspora in Australia—is a writer, poet, human rights lawyer, and academic. She has worked and published in the fields of sexual violence and impunity during and post Sri Lanka's civil war; and contestation of constitutional land rights and rule of law challenges in post-war Sri Lanka. She has also worked in a pro bono capacity in refugee legal protection in Sydney. Her commentary has appeared in various news sources including *The Conversation* (Australia) and the *Colombo Telegraph* (Sri Lanka). She is inspired by the stories of the fierce courage displayed by Sri Lankan women currently in the North of Sri Lanka, but also by members of the diaspora who courageously navigate lives away from their homeland. She is grateful primarily to the women in her family—Lily, Christine, Shanti and Anthea—for this and everything else.

Ellis Island, 1918

Jennifer deBie

Three generations, and a century this year—
he was a refugee.
Blow-in from Belgium,
skin of my skin and jawline to jawbone,
my blood 'cross the water
hunting safe harbor in the promised land
while the war to end all wars
burned.'

My history book records two,
your's will remember more.

Eternity watches an Italian optician
and the recesses of Irish shop doors,
and the tents raised on grit for those who wait,
a step on a journey unwanted.

My father told me there are ranches at the border
with gates in fences the owners never cross.
Doors unlocked to those willing,
a landowner's promise not to impede,
and the small kindnesses of water jugs left in the desert.

Four women break fruit together,
apples taken in silence.
There is meaning
wherever women eat apples.

My mother told me she does not want grandchildren,
told me her fears for a child born into *this*—
into a white middle class
American
family, three generations and a century after
new arrival.

అ

Jennifer deBie was born and raised in Texas on the blurred ground between South and West. She has studied in Texas, spent a summer in Italy, and currently lives in Ireland where she is pursuing a PhD at University College Cork studying Mary Shelley and Frankenstein. Her work has been featured in *Little Atoms*, *Sound Historian*, and Manawaker Studios' *Starward Tales Anthology*. Her novel for young adults, *The Adventures of Dogg Girl and Sidekick*, was published by Dreaming Big Publications in 2018.

GROOTA PIETER[1]

Mitchell Toews

In 1964, my ninth summer, make-shift fruit stands lined the Number 12 Highway along its approach to Hartplatz, in Southern Manitoba. Local entrepreneurs in borrowed trucks had motored to the distant orchards of the Okanagan and back. The fruit of their labours was announced by the signs that had sprouted along the highway: Fresh! B.C. Cherries!

At their roadside stands, the sunflower-seed-cracking vendors eyed us suspiciously when we pulled up on our bikes, dimes at the ready. "No free tasting!" they would warn, wagging wary fingers at us *schnoddanäses*.

I remember seeing strangely dressed boys of about my age hanging around. They had soup bowl haircuts and wore boots that looked like they had seen some real work. Some cowshit too. Banished from the proximity of the produce they had helped pick, they roughhoused and pelted rocks at telephone poles as their fathers collected our payments.

A few weeks later when the school year began, and the playgrounds and classrooms were jammed with children scrubbed lye soap clean and wearing new clothes, I saw the cherry truck boys again. Unlike me, they did not have a new plaid pencil case and fresh-from-the-box Dash runners. They

---

[1] This is an edited version of a story that was first published online and in print by *River Poets Journal* (Summer, 2018). With thanks to the original editor and Lilly Press for permission to reprint it here.

looked and acted much as they had beside the highway. I saw them puffing on corn silk roll-your-owns in the windrow of trees along Kroeker Avenue. They gathered there like hobbits, all bony knuckles and patched denim overalls.

A shy, freckle-hided elf, I hovered nearby in curiosity. I heard them speaking Low German, which I only barely understood. A long and bickersome family history, spanning generations, shunnings, continents, and exoduses, had made English the designated language of our household.

"Who are those kids, anyway?" I asked my friend Harold as we walked home from school.

"They're from Mexico," he said, kicking a discarded Rogers Golden Syrup can.

"But they don't sound Mexican. They talk like my Opa."

"Well, yeah! They're Mennonites."

"Shouldn't they be from Russia then? Or Ukraine?"

"Not these ones." Harold shrugged. "Our Sunday School sponsors one."

My family were Mennonites too, but not much given to churchgoing. This was the first I had heard of Mexican Mennonites and sponsorships.

We played baseball at school that warm fall and it soon became apparent that while these new kids were not much for rules, they could really hit and throw. Some uneasy alliances were made but for the most part, our games were tense contests of Canadians against Mexicans. Neither label was wholly accurate, but we were kids slinging names at one another, and our political correctness had no beginning and our playground animosity knew no end.

Finally, after a scuffle broke out over a controversial fair-foul call, a Battle Royale was suggested to settle our differences. The rumble would begin as soon as school let out. Our field of glory was to be the parking lot behind the nearby Evangelical Fellowship Church. Fighting on school property meant expulsion if you were caught, and we were keen to distance ourselves from that consequence.

As we filed in for last classes—Art followed by Devotions —the *Mexikaunsche* crew looked confident. They were out-numbered three to one but seemed unconcerned. One boy poked his finger against my new corduroy jacket sleeve and said, "You're gonna really get it from Groota Pieter!" Again my Low German failed me, but even in English the phrase 'Peter the Great' meant nothing to me.

The four o'clock bell rang, and we dashed to the cloakroom to don our brave apparel and make for the battleground.

We didn't know exactly how to start. Congregated in shuf-fling clumps on opposing sides of the gravel lot, it was almost as if we needed a teacher or a pastor to organize the activity. But it was up to us to finish what we started.

"We should get garbage can lids and have a stone fight!" one of our gang suggested.

We considered this option at length. We were still weighing the relative merits of artillery versus infantry when everyone stopped talking and stared, open-mouthed, at our foes.

A boy of about six feet had joined them. He stood among them like a thin balsam growing up from a cluster of ground-hugging juniper. A lone emissary from their side strode with reckless bravado towards us, carrying a white handkerchief.

"No fair bringing a big brother!" one of our members called out.

"He ain't no brother. That's Groota Pieter. He arrived yes-terday with his Taunte Lena."

"He's too big! No fair!"

"He's twelve, but he's gonna be in grade four—in our class. He starts tomorrow."

Our side's tactical advantage was gone—escaped and bounding away like a rabbit freed from its hutch. We put our heads together as we did in our football huddles on the green grass of Barkman Park. Groota Pieter's threatening presence had inspired us to unity. Eventually, Harold spoke for us all: "fighting is against our religion anyway!" Our hasty council agreed with unanimous fervor. We voted for peace. Had we swords we would surely have beat them into ploughshares, but having only garbage can lids, we dropped them in clattering surrender.

A few days later, I made Groota Pieter my first pick for our lunch-hour ball team. He ambled over, and I fitted him with my dad's ball glove, brought in anticipation of this exact circumstance. I addressed him haltingly in my pidgin *Plautdietsch*.

"Oh, I can speak English," he said, taking his place at first base. He fixed me with a stink eye that I did not soon forget. But he could do more than glare. He could also gobble up grounders and hurl lightning bolts across the field. The game ended when he smashed the ball into Plumber Unger's garden, far beyond the schoolyard fence.

Pieter became Pete and after only a few months the differences between us did not seem important.

Many seasons after meeting Pete, I sat on the wet bleachers at my granddaughter's fastball game. We were visitors in a town not far from Hartplatz. A floor mat from my pickup truck served as a makeshift seat cushion for the late May contest. I was happy to be there. Baseball had been gone from my life for quite a few summers now and it was good to be back. I liked this old ballpark with its painted backstops, where tall ironweed stems and winding thistle grew close to the wooden planks, kindred in their effort to escape the mower's blades.

"Hey Jake, I think the rain's done for today," a man said as he climbed up to the row in front of me. He smiled at the fellow seated there and sat beside him.

The two seemed like regulars at these games. Both were about my age.

"How are you, Obram?" Jake said to the new arrival.

"Oh, it goes to hold out. You?"

"Same," Jake said, accepting a handful of sunflower seeds.

The two men cracked and spat, clearing their throats and murmuring as the teams went through their infield warm-ups on the wet diamond.

The Hartplatz team came to bat first. After the leadoff batter struck out, the next to the plate was a player I did not recognize. *Must be a new kid,* I thought.

"Oh, dis oughta be good," Obram said quietly, then yelled. "Easy out!"

I looked away as he shot a sidling glance in my direction and focused on the batter's box. The girl wore a discreet headscarf beneath her batting helmet. The scarf came up from under her uniform tunic and covered her neck and the back of her head.

"She one of them border crossers?" I heard Obram speculate. The other man shrugged and dropped his remaining seeds onto the ground.

After working the count full, the batter hit a sharp drive over second base. Her bright eyes beamed at their bench as she reached the bag.

"Pretty good hittin'," Jake said, giving me a friendly smile.

The next batter bunted, advancing her. Then my grand-daughter lined out to the pitcher to end the inning. *Right back at 'er*, I thought.

Our pitcher took the mound. It was the girl with the head-scarf. She threw hard and the home crowd watched anxiously as she struck out the side, overpowering the batters.

"She's too tall," Obram grumbled, standing. He put his hands in his pockets and turned to me. "Your pitcher—she's older den sixteen, right?" He prodded again when I did not answer. "She looks older than sixteen—but it's hard to tell with them…"

"Well, if that's the rule, I'm sure she's no more than sixteen. She's new on the team."

"New?" snorted Obram. "I bet. Where's she from, any-way?"

"Corner of Friesen Avenue and First, I think." This won me a small chuckle from Jake.

"Eh? Whatever," Obram said. He returned his attention to the game, clapping his hands.

Several innings passed, and the game remained scoreless. Both pitchers were throwing well. As the game progressed, it became apparent that the men hunched in front of me were deep in conversation. It did not seem altogether friendly and they had forgotten about baseball.

Cold, I hurried back to fetch a jacket from the truck. When I returned, Obram and Jake had left the bleachers and were standing on the edge of the parking lot. Their posture and raised voices told me something was wrong.

"Well, we grew up in a 'sanctuary city' too!" Jake said, his face red. "When our folks left Russia, Manitoba gave us land, a home! Our parents were refugees too, yours and mine—ev-eryone in their village."

"Those were different times," Obram sputtered. "Our people came in peace!"

"Acch. Same manure, different pile!" Jake replied with disdain.

"Nay, nay!" Obram said. "Besides, nobody really gave us nothing! We worked the land, cleared it and picked rocks—it was just scrub brush before we came!"

"It was Métis land before we came! They had the deeds. The government promised to compensate them, but they took years, and never paid *nuscht*! Dragged their feet. Did you know that?" Jake fought to maintain his composure, kicking at a patch of crumbling asphalt as he spoke. "The Métis scattered eventually. We pushed them off. Never did seem right to me."

Obram lit a cigarette and held it in a cupped hand while he thought, his head bowed. "Our families feared God and wanted nothing but to live together without war. Can these illegals say the same? They're terrorists!" He faltered, realizing that he was shouting.

By then I was listening intently. Their clash was the sort of thing you read online but seldom hear out loud, between two men so like each other and both so like me. I had forgotten this was a place just north of the U.S. border, on the front lines of refugee traffic. Unsettled, I went back to the bleachers.

After twenty minutes, with the game still scoreless in the last inning, Jake returned wearing a wool Mackinaw. He took the same spot, just in front of me. As the teams switched places on the field, he looked over. "Sorry about Obram. He's a loud-mouth but he doesn't usually get so outta line."

"It's a tough situation," I said.

"Maybe. For me, it's clear-cut. Our family settled here at first, then migrated to Mexico. We ended up moving back here in the '60s. Not everyone was friendly when we arrived. I know what it's like."

I nodded, hiding my guilt. "You say the sixties?"

"Yeah. Christmas, 1964. I didn't speak a word of English when we got here."

Just then, the tall girl with the headscarf hit a long fly ball. With one out, the runner on third tagged up and trotted in with the first run.

"Well, how about that! Looks like the visitors are making it interesting," Jake said with a wink.

"They always do."

Mitchell Toews lives on the shore of a Manitoba lake where he is writing a novel set in the same boreal forest that surrounds him. He also produces short stories and flash fiction for readers in Canada, the U.S., the UK, and Australia. The letters in his Grade 1 Reader spoke to Mitch—so clearly—each with its own distinct personality; letting him in on their secret kingdom. Fifty-some years later, he's all gristle and scar but those little letters still look up and wink. When an insufficient number of *We are pleased to inform you...* emails are on hand, he finds alternative joy in the windy intermingling between the top of the water and the bottom of the sky, or skates on the ice until he can no longer see the cabin.

Mitch's writing has appeared in a number of literary journals in Canada, the U.S., and the UK. Details can be found at his website: Mitchellaneous.com

CHALICE

Judith Skillman

Thin sun on daffodils.
Cup raised to the absent dreams of night.
Groundskeeper goes about his reversals.
Moss usurps patio stones, twigs cover
over this place where grief—
the salt-taste of grief, lies submerged in spring.

Tamp it down, push it back, keep it at bay.
You are only leaving the place you came to love.
You are the one refugee, immigrant, emigrant
who never came to find a home
in any of the myriad houses
you occupied. You with your orange-teas

and cups of half-drunk milk,
pills laid out in ovals on odalisque-shaped bars.
Your greening willow gone,
and the fireflies, for whom the sun
was just a small bulb attached
to one part of the body.

That it could come and go at will—
that childhood would never end, and,
with it, the hot scalding tears
flowing after a beating, a reprimand, an accident
of jumping the fence
to palm a shard of glass.

❧

Judith Skillman's recent book is *Kafka's Shadow* (Deerbrook Editions, 2017). Her poems have appeared in many journals, including *Cimarron Review*, *Shenandoah*, *Hawai'i Review*, and *J Journal*, and in anthologies, including *Nasty Women Poets* (Lost Horse Press). She has been a writer in residence at the Centrum Foundation, and is the recipient of a 2017 Washington Trust GAP grant. Visit: www.judithskillman.com; jkpaintings.com; https://www.facebook.com/judith.skillman.

THE ART OF MIGRATION AND THE COURAGE TO CREATE

A PERSONAL REFLECTION

Virginia Ryan

I am an Australian/Italian binational visual artist trained in Canberra, Australia. Since the eighties, I have lived and worked in varied countries: Egypt, Brazil, Serbia, Scotland, Ivory Coast, and Ghana in West Africa. I completed post-graduate studies in Art Therapy in Edinburgh, Scotland after moving there from war-torn ex-Yugoslavia in 1994. For a time, affected by so much violence, I questioned my position as an image-maker. Yet in all of the places I have lived, I have engaged with other artists and kept my practice alive; risk-taking, at times failing, experimenting, but always continuing.

For as long as I can remember, I have been interested in questions of boundaries, from the edge of a scrap of paper to fences, walls and shorelines; sites that may cause us to experience inclusion-exclusion, belonging or separateness; the excitement of discovering what lies inside or on the other side; the misery of remaining "outside," and the security of being held within. Safe places, refuges; forbidding places, exclusion zones.

Mine has been a peripatetic life, yet lived with intention.

Without these voyages, my recent encounters with refugees in Italy would perhaps not have occurred so spontaneously. I too am one who has migrated, who lives in a country far from that of my birth; yet I'm acutely aware that my travel and boundary-crossings have been facilitated by white privilege and economic security.

In 2016 I returned 'home' to central Italy—an area known for wines, truffles, olive oil, and a Christian spiritual heritage interwoven with Medieval and Renaissance painting and architecture. For millennia, this place has been a destination for pilgrims and travelers from North, South, East and West. Since 2000, I had been living mostly in Ghana and Ivory Coast, interspersed with brief periods in Umbria. After having absorbed so much around me and having produced much art in my West African studios, I now embarked on creating a new body of work connecting Africa and Europe: shields incorporating the ancient female practice of threading, knotting and weaving materials—photographs, scraps of *pagne* fabrics and old Italian embroideries, found objects and threads. *Objects-trouvees*, disregarded and abandoned and considered waste, had formed part of many of my previous installations since 2000. The notion of cura—from the Latin *cura/curae*: to take care, pay attention, to heal—in respect of the *abandoned* is a personally important consideration. From here comes the term "curator" used in contemporary art practice; I felt both creator and curator of these works. While deeply engaged in my practice, I missed West Africa: the vibrancy and talent; the boundless stimulation of street life; the welcome—if at times exhausting—assault on the senses; and the youthful demographics.

꙳

The organisation that came to be known as *Make Art Not Walls/Italia* grew from an initial encounter with a group of refugees arriving from sub-Saharan West African countries in September 2016. They were living temporarily in my home town of Trevi.

Unlike me, these new arrivals did not have passports and visas. They were waiting on the outcome of their applications for residency, which can take years—a precarious situation that was felt strongly. They had embarked on arduous journeys across the Sahara and had found themselves spending months—or indeed years—in Libya's forced migrant camps. Felix, one of the young men whom I had the privilege of meeting, and who is still making art in his new home in Perugia, had escaped slavery after having being sold; others had payed ransoms to camp guards; and all had bought places on dinghies or small boats for the perilous sea crossing. Some, like Raphael, did not know that the boat he clambered onto in the dead of night in Libya would be landing in Italy. All were young. All were traumatised and yet resilient as only the young can be.

Our first encounter occurred seemingly by chance. I noticed a group of men walking up and down the main road whilst I was driving past, through the valley below Trevi. After a few days, it dawned on me that they were not passers-by en route to somewhere else, and my curiosity was piqued. I sought information in the council offices and learnt that the city had recently agreed to host around fifty men and women who had disembarked in Sicily before being bussed to various reception centres throughout the Italian mainland.

Through Arci, an Italian NGO, I made contact with staff at the Trevi refugee reception centre—a transformed, slightly decrepit hotel—and extended an invitation to the local museum where recent work from my series, "I Will Shield You" was on display. I felt strongly that there might be interest, and a sense of recognition, of the African content if these young men and women were to see the exhibition; I was not disappointed.

When the moment arrived that September day, a van with ten or so young adults climbed out, stepping into a museum for the first time with no apparent sense of unease. Everything was new to them, both positive and negative; for the time being, I assumed, they felt safe after having been adrift for months. For them, the centuries-old frescoes, *ex-votos*, and my contemporary shields were a wonderland of complex, interrelated images in a new but non-threatening environment. None spoke Italian and the francophones from Mali and Ivory Coast could not speak to the anglophone Ghanians, Gambians, and Nigerians (although at times there may be a cross-over autochthonous language); yet all of us understood a common visual language there in the local museum.

The young men and women seemed enthusiastic to see the work that referenced my West African experience. They stood close, peering into each elaborate artwork and thus allowing an intimate encounter between viewers and objects. I was equally enthusiastic to chat with people who had recently experienced their own personal Odysseys, and who appeared keen to share their stories with someone who was familiar with their homelands. At the end of that first afternoon it was suggested I should go and visit them in their space: their first Italian home.

It was to be the beginning of an intense two year period of connection through image-making, resulting in exhibitions locally and internationally in Italy, Edinburgh, and Los Angeles; with talks and presentations in local schools; and a large body of work that documents the history and identity of the group and individual participants.

My first visit to the centre was tentative and exploratory; it was generous on both sides. I still remember walking in with a ball of red string, some pencils and paper on that breezy October afternoon, not knowing what to expect, being open. It was that day we named the group *Make Art Not Walls*. From the very start, our communal approach explored the power of visual imagery to aid in healing the traumatic life experiences that had shaken the cores of these young men and women. Previous drawing skills were not required or expected; what was hoped for was the courage to create, even for the first time, in a non-judgmental environment.

The discovery of a personal visual narrative involves risk-taking and trust for both beginner image-makers and experienced artists. The participants had already shown courage through the very fact of having undertaken the dangerous voyage to Italy. From day one, our common aim was to become intimate with the notion of courage, derived from the latin root *cor*, meaning *heart*: the commonly perceived seat of the emotions. The word courage traditionally intended "to speak by telling one's heart." Trust was perhaps harder; having been mishandled and abused, slighted and treated as rubbish, the refugees needed time to regain faith in their fellow humans.

Our mission was to build upon a foundation of courage and to nurture a sense of self through a human-centred approach; we held that each person, given space and time, has the potential to work through trauma and stress to find a new sense of self. The time of waiting—of waiting for documents, of waiting for something to happen—perceived often as passive and pointless, might become, to some degree, a time of exploration and growing self-awareness. A time to prepare for the next step on an arduous journey. As one of the participants said: for him, "being a migrant can also mean becoming a new person; the person I hope to be."

After the first, tentative encounters in the dining area of the refugee accommodation centre, a crucial workspace—a room of our own—was provided in a disused garage, so that participants could have twenty four hour access to basic, donated art supplies and recycled materials. From the beginning, the keys were kept by nominated participants who managed the room autonomously. For those of us involved, something quite magical happened in that space: an unfolding of potential. Looking back, we experienced an almost utopian sense of the power of our group and of each individual to create a cosmopolitan microcosm within which an appreciation of diversity, and the unique qualities of each member, was held in consideration and became the grammar of our time together. Yes, there were misunderstandings, arguments, and resistances from all sides. At the same time, there was always a will to break through, and to make something of value.

Our first public exhibition of works was in December 2016, in one of the spaces at the local museum where we had first met. The museum thus became even more important to the group; a place of reflection and observation, of learning, and of contact with Italy's history, as well as a place to meet sympathetic long term residents and foreign visitors. This exhibition of works-in-progress was to become our default *modus operandi*: being present as a collective in public spaces, and demonstrating to the community at large evidence of creative activity, with the intention of building a bridge between recent immigrants and other residents. Taking the work outside the confines of the art-room also validated the importance of the creative act in the eyes of the participants themselves, who witnessed the responses of the public.

The artworks reflected the instability and transitory nature of the refugees' status, and the short duration of their stay in Umbria. Many, however, showed an exciting level of engagement and graphic and pictorial development, and slowly, over time, a number of the most committed participants began visually to narrate their harrowing voyage across the Sahara in more and more detail. It was important for this to happen before the memories receded; for even this trauma, one day, would seem a long way away.

Other new participants joined us after they arrived at the accommodation centre over the period until May 2018; some created their first works on paper or wood, and continued with trepidation or enthusiasm, and sometimes a combination of the two; others came, looked around, and left never to return. Whilst we encouraged conversation and experimentation, the group was always voluntary; some remained sceptical.

Overall, the small-sized yet numerous works often depicted memories of home, of time spent in detention centres in Libya, the voyage across the Mediterranean, hopes for the future, and heart-felt dreams of a new life in Europe. The depictions surprised by their tenderness; by the yearnings for a place to call home, for children, and a deeply romantic love-life. Such renderings co-existed with graphic paintings of crouched bodies in car boots, men behind prison bars in Libya, and the emotional arrival in Sicily.

Most of the works were produced by men, as the few women involved in the group were moved to another reception centre one day in August 2017. I was deeply concerned that they were no longer with us; yet as volunteers we had no control over such decision-making. A strong commitment to the empowerment of women had been a defining feature of our group's approach; this process was disrupted by their unexpected departure. We were also committed to religious freedom and openness of declared sexual orientation. While over the course of two years, none of the fifty men who participated declared himself to be homosexual, I made sure that it was clear that there would be total acceptance on the part of the volunteers should anyone choose to come out. Even so, I was aware that it was highly improbable in an all-male, West African environment that anyone would feel ready to do so. We all visited exhibitions—such as that of gay artist Franko B—where issues around gender and sexual orientation were discussed in an art context. There were a number of Gambians who may have left Gambia as a result of the country's persecution of gay people. My approach was to create a safe place, allowing people to imagine that one day a sense of freedom might allow such opening; but never did I feel a right, or any need, to push further. At times, tentative images seemed to be telling us something; if the group had continued, personal breakthroughs about sexual orientations may have continued.

Our group valued not only the refugee participants, but also the volunteers who supported these young men. As volunteers we learnt from our involvement, and grew in understanding and appreciation of the experience of displacement. Some of the refugee participants became friends and at times offered us, in turn, their support and friendly advice. Being an artist myself, I encouraged everyone involved to feel free to think, paint, and draw outside the box, but always from within a framework of respect and nonviolence.

One of the questions I asked myself, and still do, is what must it have been like for these young people, after months of travel, of violence, and of abuse and fear, to be in a room full of colour, music, and conversation, where the shame many expressed was replaced by a sense of experimentation and encouragement. A place to transition, to prepare themselves emotionally for the next part of the journey: receiving or not receiving work documents, being integrated, or perhaps becoming outcasts again – if refused asylum or humanitarian protection – for this too happens in Europe, and very often.

Alex, Souleymane, Blessing, Raphael, Abubacar, Isaia, Ernest, Festus, Sannah, Foday and *Lucky.* Some of the names that became so well known to me, and to the local supporters who came together with us, despite a pervasive mistrust—fuelled by negative press—in many local residents.

The day the centre was shut down without prior warning—7th of May, 2018—is scratched into my soul: a violent memory of men once again being displaced, moved on to other reception centres in Umbria; of men becoming just names on a piece of paper. Like waste, hidden from us in garbage dumps and landfill, the migrant is often "processed" as unwanted material to be hidden from view, disregarded. After our friends' departure, I was shocked that so few local people asked us where they had gone or what had happened, despite the fact that the group had been living in the area for two years. So they became ghosts in a way, and we were left bereft and feeling as if most of our fellow citizens preferred it that way; a deeply disturbing lesson that I am still processing.

The other volunteers and I remain in contact with many of those who were removed, and we have encouraged them to set up their own groups; some are still painting, and we are still publishing small books of their images and texts in Italian. With the consensus of the group members, I was made guardian of the many artworks left in our art-room when it was dismantled that afternoon. I have negotiated with the city authorities to have them hung as a permanent installation in the local House of Culture that is soon to open. As one former participant, Alex, said to me with pride: "One day, when I have a job and a family here in Italy, I will come back to see the works again and tell my children I was part of that; that we were the people to tell these stories."

❧

Virginia Ryan is an Australian-Italian binational artist/art therapist working in Europe and West Africa who studied at the Florence University of Foreigners, the National Art School, Canberra, Australia and Queen Margaret School of Art Therapy in Edinburgh, Scotland. Ryan co-founded the ongoing Foundation for Contemporary Art (FCA) in Ghana, which she directed until 2007, and the association Make Art Not Walls/Italia with asylum seekers in 2016 in Umbria, Italy. She exhibits internationally. For further information, visit: www.virginiaryan.com

The Man Who Talks to Birds

Enesa Mahmić

Once in a forest park
I met a stranger, feeding the birds.
Last sunset of the dying autumn
Mirrored in his eyes.
He told me:

"Dear friend,
My English is almost incomprehensible
I can't talk to people
I'm just sitting on this bench and speaking with the birds."

The Map and the Migrant

Sharif Gemie

Abdul passed Kateb a sheet of paper. "It's from Mohammad," he whispered. "He's got to Milan!" Kateb glanced round the little café, worried that everyone was looking at them. Instead, the old men continued to play dominoes; the two Iraqis, sitting together, looked at their mobile phone; the Turkish workers sipped their coffee and blew cigarette smoke into the air. No one looked, no one cared.

Kateb unfolded the paper. The sketch was an extraordinary sight, drawn with amateurish enthusiasm, full of Mohammad's childlike delight in the world. It showed a little stick figure following a route across seas, towns, and borders, catching buses, taxis, trains, and boats. At each stage Mohammad had added comments: "Ask for Raj. Do not trust anyone else… Offer twenty-five euros, but be prepared to pay thirty-five… Hamzi will sell you a life-jacket. Insist on an orange one…Buy bread and water at the Silver Star café…"

The little stick man moved before Kateb's eyes like a cartoon figure: it jumped happily over frontiers, skipped over waves, slipped through cafés. It whizzed along, always smiling, infected by Mohammad's cheerfulness…in a word, blessed. Could he travel like this? wondered Kateb. Could he be like this stick man, waving a little Syrian flag as he arrived in Milan?

Kateb gazed over the grey sea. His life had become straight-forward: everything depended on one simple action. With his mind and body he concentrated on gripping the side of the boat. Hold on. Hold on. He had lost everything else: his wife, his daughters, his laptop, his suitcase, his money, his identity card. His mobile phone no longer worked: maybe it was just damp, maybe it was broken. He had a few Turkish coins left in the pocket of his coat. And that was all. No, not all. He still had Mohammad's map, carefully folded in his inside pocket. And he had an email address. If he got to Greece, he would email his family.

Kateb was uncomfortable. He was twisted unpleasantly, his legs and lower torso crammed into the mass of people surrounding him, his upper torso forced over the edge of the boat and facing towards the sea. He looked to the horizon, trying to spot the blue inflatable that was carrying his wife Karima and his two daughters. It was out there somewhere, it had to be. With his left hand he clutched the side of the boat. His right hand, balled up into a fist, pressed onto his coat, onto the map inside, onto his heart.

The old wooden boat was crowded, indeed over-crowded. Sixty or so cold, damp, desperate-looking men were jammed into every inch of the surface, most sitting round the edge, some—less lucky—pushed into the middle. Some wore bright orange life-jackets, some wore blue life-jackets, some had none. In an emergency, how many would work? wondered Kateb. Another wave rocked the boat, a thick, slow, dangerous swell. The men swayed, pushing one against another, shouting in alarm in Kurdish, in Arabic, in Farsi. "Careful, careful!" cried the thin teenager next to him, clutching with extra force to the side of the boat. A chorus of prayers and oaths followed: some blessed God for keeping them safe, others cursed the boat-owner, the traffickers, and the fat man at the stern, the rod of the engine in his hand. "Don't blame me!" he shouted, "I don't control the waves."

A ripple of laughter went round, but it was weak and uncertain. The fat man had been forced into his position by armed traffickers. He swore. "Take this thing!" he pleaded, looking at the other travellers. "Please: take it." No one responded: all eyes were on the sea, measuring the height of the next thick, slow swell and the inches of the boat above the water. The engine coughed and spluttered with an irregular rhythm, leaving an unpleasant oily smell that stuck in their throats. It reminded them that they hadn't eaten for twelve hours and that precious little water was left. It was simple, Kateb told himself. Hold on. Hold on. And keep the map. That was all.

Mohammad's map wasn't wrong, thought Kateb, it wasn't inaccurate. But it wasn't *his* map; that was the problem. What would his map look like? It had been dictated to him by polite but ineffective charities; hostile, arbitrary border guards; and profiteering traffickers. His stick man would be hunched, burdened, unhappy. The line of his journey would be marked by zigzags, sudden halts, and meandering, confused trajectories. Instead of leaping over borders, his stick man would bounce back from them. Old fishing boats, unsafe dinghies, and Italian rescue ships had traced out his erratic journey

71

westwards, leading here, to Malta. At least Karima and the girls had survived. A blessing! At least there was that.

He glanced round to Des, the smartly-dressed Nigerian sitting next to him, the one who still looked like a yuppie after braving deserts, bandit gangs in Libya, corrupt officials, and criminal traffickers. His powder blue suit was spotless: how did he do that? Des had told him that in other holding centres the refugees had been transferred after three or four days. Here, in Malta, they'd been held for three weeks. No one knew why, or when they might be transferred. "Des?" he asked politely, in English. "What is the time?" Des smiled. This was the fifth time that Kateb had asked the question in the past hour. He reached into the inside pocket of his impeccable jacket, pulled out his mobile, and told him: 2:53. "I will go to see Karima," Kateb said, almost as if he was asking permission. Des nodded, and smiled. He knew Kateb's habits, the patterns he'd developed while waiting in the holding centre.

Kateb walked along the corridor, past little groups of men talking, whispering, propped up against the wall. For reasons he didn't understand, they congregated here to do deals and exchange rumours. At first sight, they looked like experienced traders: the gravity with which they spoke, their careful hand gestures, and the way they lowered their voices as Kateb approached suggested that they were discussing important matters. But he knew otherwise. They were debating ten cigarettes for a broken mobile, which could be cannibalized for parts; two euros for a mostly unused notebook, not very damaged by sea water; ten euros for a meeting with a man who knew someone with a connection to a boat-owner. He sighed, turned through the doors, down the dark little staircase, and into the bright Mediterranean sunlight.

Down by the fence, the elderly Iraqi Sufi was keeping order. Pressed against the wires was a group of men, dressed in the ill-fitting greys, browns, and blacks of the holding centre. They shouted over the space that separated their compound from the women's and children's compound. When they got out of hand, the Sufi would admonish them: "Brothers, brothers…" In times of great stress, he'd chant verses from the Koran, his voice deep, resonant, but not entirely in tune. Kateb came here every day at three to see Karima, who sometimes brought the children.

"Brother," the Sufi appealed to the Afghan engineer, "give way to our Syrian friend." Kateb had asked Des if this separation of the sexes was normal in European holding centres. "Normal?" Des had replied. "Normal? Do you think anything in our lives is normal?" Hold on, Kateb told himself. He grasped the fence. There was Karima walking towards him with his two smiling daughters. Hold on.

৵

Sharif Gemie is a retired history professor. He used to write about themes such as minorities and cross-cultural contacts. His most recent non-fiction work is *The Hippy Trail: A History*. After retirement, he turned to creative writing as he thought it was time to do some real work. Writing about fictional cross-cultural contacts and journeys is a logical continuation of his historical research. "The Map and the Migrant" was inspired by a copy of a map drawn by a real-life migrant. Sharif is half-Egyptian: he grew up in London and has lived in Wales for twenty five years.